Flog
A dead horse

Poetry Anthology

Musa Gift Masombuka

Thabile Sekgobela

Thabang Tshwane

Thabang Makgenepye Aphane

Mapule Octovia Pila

Lesego Daniel Kgwete

Josiah Molokoane

authorHOUSE®

AuthorHouse™ LLC
1663 Liberty Drive
Bloomington, IN 47403
www.authorhouse.com
Phone: 1-800-839-8640

Published by AuthorHouse   03/18/2014

ISBN: 978-1-4918-4959-0 (sc)
ISBN: 978-1-4918-4960-6 (e)

Library of Congress Control Number: 2014900480

Contents

Introduction

Have you felt stressed, depressed, sad, jubilant or feeling lonely? Have you been betrayed, heartbroken, back-stabbed or defeated? Have you ever been challenged or felt like the world has neglected you, all sorts of love has faded within you? Have you ever experienced your dreams becoming your worst nightmares, feeling useless? This book will help you restore and rebuild your confidence. It is said that things seem impossible until they are done.

In this book you will find all kinds of poems, some of them you may think that they are criticizing you or against your culture. But no hard feelings because poetry is well written with facts hidden between the lines, it seem a bit challenging because it tells about love, fight, hatred, negligence, friendship, romance and flash-backs.

People use to think that only experts do better but what they don't know is that they all start from the bottom. Those who lack self-confidence and those who need facts-of-life, this book will guide you. To those who are heart-broken, faded trust and lonely in life, we've got poems to show you the light.

Some people prefer poems with only author name. Well, in this book is different, we cover author biographies, poems and questions to test your understanding of poetry. This book has been written by 7 secondary school pupils expressing their love for poetry. It has been written with various different themes and languages. It is suitable for secondary schools where English is their home language or second language.

Poetry is more than just putting words on a paper to express the inner feelings right from your heart. The poets have used hidden but comprehensible language to express their feelings so that when going through the poem, it goes right through to the bones from your heart to jiggle your body. Poetry ever since introduced it has been divided into genres like; prison poetry, lyric poetry, legendary poetry, Shakespeare, millennium poetry and oral poetry.

MISSION

To provide knowledge to the people about poetry. To empower the nation through learning, Flog A Dead Horse Poetry Anthology is a book which covers author biographies for people to know about the life of an author, and a short description about the poem to make the poem more simple and understandable. No glossary included in this book, learners should inherit the characteristics of students of doing researches for themselves, never always rely on a teacher for everything.

VISION

Explore the world of poetry. Bring poetry back to life from the cold depths. To see learners understanding poetry in plural. To see learners being educated, mind-enriched, self-dependant and teacher independent on everything.

Biographies of the poets

Musa Gift Masombuka (autobiography).

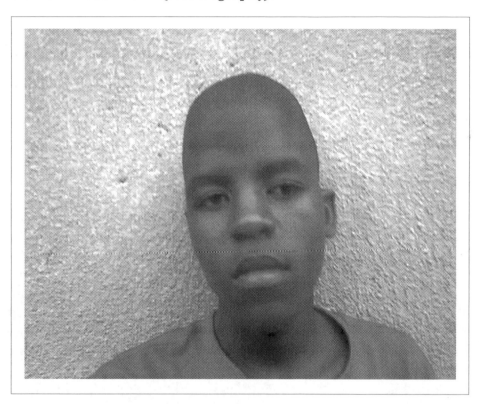

About Musa Gift Masombuka.

I was born 1 April 1998, the first son of Anna Masombuka and Vusi Sibiya followed by an illegitimate Charlie Oratile Masombuka. I was born and bred in Siyabuswa with the Sibiya family until age 2, I enrolled a crech pre-owned by Gogo Betty Sibiya. Due to relationship difficulties and conflicts between my father and mom, 2000 I moved back to live with Masombuka family until present. I migrated to Tsantsabela (Regae Township) with Masombuka family in 2000 and I had to learn new life and language.

Schooling.

I enrolled at Regae Primary School as a creche pupil in 2000 and I graduated in 2003 towards end. 2004 I enrolled in Mohlahlane Primary School until I graduated my last grade (Grade 7) in 2010 end. In 2011 I enrolled at Majatladi Secondary school as a grade 8 learner and currently still at Grade 11. In 2013 November I attended the New Arizona Computer training school and I graduated from it in December.

Health.

I am not a healthy person, to be honest with you. I am a boy who suffered from server brain seizures and many children illnesses. I had a breathing difficulty infection (Asthma) since age 3 and I have been on medication treatment until now.

Family Backgrounds.

Not much more I would say but I will tell the little that I know. Ever since I opened my eyes to start understanding things of this world, I didn't have one father. All along my life had been surrounded by step-fathers in this broken family game. My mother is someone bossy and doesn't like telling facts of life or discuss anything with children, she always think that children don't understand. It hurt me the most after I found out that my biological father passed away after a sudden illness, she told me very late. There was a wall between the Sibiya and Masombuka family, well and I am their sword to defend themselves. Feud is what I've been experiencing. I was an orphan before time, I never felt either motherly or fatherly love. There are secrets between the walls and conspiracy in the family, I am living my life on questions . . . Wondering that what is it more that they are not telling me? They accuse good people for their mistakes. They always say 'It was for your own good.' How will the issue of not knowing my father benefit me because it will only hurt me?. Meanwhile the late Vusi Sibiya had 2 daughters which are also illegitimate to me namely: Nomfundo and Ntokozo.

This issue just had a soft spot in my heart, when I think about it I would just weep. I wonder what went wrong after my born? Am I the beautiful sinner to unite enemies? In english it is always said that 'First born babies are mostly mistakes.' maybe I was never meant to be. All along I've been living a lie until last year 2013 where I got a chance to know my roots, it was special yet too late because many have fallen in this life adventure, they were no longer with us.

Well . . . Masombuka family is a very strict and a fantasy family. Witchcraft is what they believe in most, which it gets me frustrated sometimes. They are caring but very secretive. And as for the Sibiya family I can't tell you much because between me and them there is a mending wall. I mean even now I am forbidden to go and see them. Why is that? They would like to play the parent part in me but Masombuka's doesn't want anything to do with them. Really? What is the war about? Go and ask them.

Favourites.

I like music especially those with messages. Songs of artists like Nicki Minaj and Miley Cyrus. I like reading poetry, novels and plays. So I learned a lot before I wrote this book. Education is my number one priority. I am an indoor person yet an extrovert. I am eager to know what's happening all over the world. Internet is my daily activity, following celebrity trends and gossips is what I like.

Book writing. (Why started to write poetry book?)

Well . . . This book is a reflection of me. All the poems in here which are written by me, I wrote them about my real life. I had too much thinking and stress in my head so before they led me to something dangerous I decided to let them out on poetry. What I am trying to stress on my poems is that 'Never ever ever and ever again keep a child distant from where he/she belongs. Because if he/she finds out, you don't know how will the reaction be.' The poem *"An Anonymous Dad"* I wrote it being in grade 8, asking myself that will I ever get the chance to meet my dad before our time is run out? Unfortunately I met him after life removed all the innocence. Thereafter the situation affected me emotionally and socially and these two poems came to mind, 1. *"To my father."* 2. *"To my father II."*
I was excruiciated I didn't know how to express this feeling of knowing a father after such a long time. Well . . . . As for the poem *Fatherless Me, Motherless I.* I wrote it because I felt like an orphan in the presence of my mother.

I guess that's all about me . . . If you would like to know me more better this autobiography has all the right information.

Lesego Daniel Kgwete. (1996-04-20).

The first son of Nurse and France Kgwete. From Tsantsabela in the outskirts of Marble Hall. He was born and bred here in Tsantsabela. He is someone who likes playing soccer and listening music to quote facts-of-life from various songs and that's what gives him courage to bottle out his feelings onto poetry. He is an introvert and doesn't like to talk much. He is comprehensible when speaking and he is always in a company of his friends.

Mapule Octovia Pila (1997-10-03)

The first and last daughter of Ivah Pila and Jacob Digomo. Mapule likes childish life, growing up for her it's like a trap. She likes playing with kids and has big dreams and missions about her future and would one day like to change the state of her family.

Thabang Makgenepye Aphane (1997-05-06).

Thabang was born and bred in Tsantsabela also known as Regae. Attended school at Mohlahlane Primary until grade 7. Moved to Seshego to enroll grade 8 at Taxila High school. He is a young talented boy who believes he can do anything, he is a rapper, poet, goal-keeper and currently studying piano. He is a true christian and believes that everything is possible. He likes science and has an inquisitive mind towards the world, to know everything about anything.

Thabile Sekgobela (1997-10-31)

The second son out of 3 of Peggy and Jimmy Sekgobela. He loves science and believes that it will take him to green pastures one day. He lies to stay fit, so he plays soccer if he gets the chance to. He is like a glue on a paper when it comes to books. He is a shy person yet likes to talk, those who know him well calls him 'Thabile the lecture'. He likes sharing amusement with his friends and family. He has a soft spot for his siblings because they make him feel at home. He likes the phrase 'If you do nothing and say nothing you will be nothing.' that's what inspires him.

Thabang Tshwane. (1998-03-03)

First son out of 2 of Welhemina and Michael Tshwane. He grew up in Tsantsabela and currently still lives at, where he is still attending school. He is a very short tempered person. He likes reading and writing but that ain't his number 1 priority. He is a quiet person and a girl taking 'bout but he isn't interested. He wishes to further his studies and explore the world.

Josiah Molokoane. (1993-09-05)

The fourth son out of 5 children of Lucy and Alphious Molokoane. He grew up here in Tsantsabela and matriculated at Gatang Comprehensive school. He is an inquisitive person and talkative. He is currently a student at T.U.T. He likes reading and exercising to keep him healthy and safe from diseases.

1

A Backstabber

By: Thabile Sekgobela

This poem I wrote after a friend of mine from childhood whom I trusted so much turns out that he is my enemy. He portrayed me and bad-mouth me . . . I realised it too late that my true friend was my backstabber.

One thing I thought about you,
You wanted to stab me at the back,
I thought we were cronies,
I thought we were a flesh in blood,
But what you did,
You stabbed me at the back,

I thought we had something in common,
You wanted to steal my image,
You wanted to steal my belongings,
It took time for me to know what you were up to,

You are a wolf in sheep's clothing,
I lost my nerve with you,
Inside of you, you are an imp,
I am hoping against hope,
That you be a better boy again.

ACTIVITIES(QUESTIONS)

1. What happened to the poet?
2. What is a crony?
3. What is a backstabber?
4. List 2 things that the backstabber did to the poet.
5. Why did it take a long time for the poet to see what his friend was up to?
6. Explain this.
   a) Imp.
   b) Lost your nerve.
   c) Hoping against hope.

2

A Half of Me

By: Lesego Kgwete

Recently after few apologies to my girlfriend and she keep turning me down. This poem just came through, I felt like a part of me was taken away because I and her shared so much within our love. So I was begging her to come back.

A half of me is something important to me,
A half of me is what keeps me alive,
A half of me is what you see,
A half of me is how I survive,
A half of me is what makes me to stay focused,
A half of me is what I thought
I would never lose,

A half of me is what I have,
A half of me is what completes my whole,
A half of me is a part of me,
A half of me is what you took,

My heart is a semi-circle,
Come back in my life so that,
I will be complete.

ACTIVITIES(QUESTIONS)

1. According to you, what is the poet's *"half of me"*?
2. A half of me what you see. Who is this half?
3. A half of me is how I survive. How?
4. A half of me is what I thought I would never lose. Who is the other half?
5. The poet without his girlfriend, he is incomplete. Quote from the poem to support this.
6. Now my heart is a semi-circle. What does it tell you about the state of the poet?
7. Why does the poet needs his half back?

3

A Hero was Born

By: Lesego Kgwete

This time I get to honour Nelson Mandela for what he has done. Deep down it touched me to see how free South Africa is today. To him I salute with this poem.

When South Africa was under a dark cloud,
When the blacks were fought for their land,
When everything was under white government,
When what is said by blacks was a cliche,
When the culture of South Africans was down the drain,

Swords were used . . .
Forcing Africans to use Afrikaans as their language,
The names of our great grandfathers . . . .
Were changed by the officials,
Because what they heard was music to their ears,
But then a hero was born in 1918,
A hero who puts his life in danger,
Inorder to change the world,
A hero who strove for freedom,
A hero who never gave up.

Nelson Rolihlahla Mandela,
The icon of the world,
He is honoured for what he did for us . . .
To live freely as birds,
A hero who spent 27years in jail,
67years to change the world,
He removed a dark cloud upon South Africa,
Since then, South Africa is a happy united county.
And that makes me proudly South African.

ACTIVITIES(QUESTIONS)

1. Before this hero, how was South Africa?
2. What is a dark cloud?
3. What is a cliche?
4. What are swords?(give example).
5. Why were the names of our great grandfathers changed by the officials?
6. Music to my ears.
   a) What figure of speech is this?
   b) What is metaphor?
7. Briefly describe this hero.
8. What is the name of the hero?
9. He is stated as the icon of the world. True or False? Why?
10. What benefit did he offer to South Africa?
11. What makes the poet proudly South African?
12. If it was you, would you have done all this for the safety of your country? Why?
13. How is South Africa today?
14. Name any 2 things named after this hero.
15. What is his date of birth?
16. What did he demand after what he has done for his country?

4

A Real Man

By: Lesego Kgwete

Well . . . Now time for that man out there. This poem I wrote it after experiencing that most men doesn't care much when it comes to brotherly love and fatherly love. I urge them to take action and responsibility.

A real man is someone who listens,
And accept whatever comes the way.
A real man is someone who has a warm hand,
And a courageous shadow,
A real man is someone who is loyal to everyone.

A real man is someone,
Who carries the tears of others on his shoulders.
A real man is someone, who is committed to every challenge,
A real man is someone who is brave,
And who risks his life for others.

A real man faces any music,
A real man survives any situation,
A real man never gives up,
A real man is a real man.

ACTIVITIES(QUESTIONS)

1. Briefly describe a real man.
2. A real man is someone who has a courageous shadow.
   -True or False? Why?
3. A real man carries the tears of others on his shoulder. How?
4. A real man is brave. Really?
5. A real man survives any situation. How does he cope?
6. A real man never_____.
7. A real man faces the music.
   a) Explain this in your own words.
   b) What figure of speech is this?
8. Quote 3 words that best describes a real man.

5

Across the River

By: Thabile Sekgobela

Across the river, is a life journey. It can be compared to the challenges we meet in life and deal with them to be successful and enjoy the lifetime while still exist.

Things won't go as well as you like,
Walking through the river,
Life was too short,
My hair was on fire,
Making bad decisions,
You will have common imagery,

Across the river,
I had too many decisions in my head,
I had a bad feeling to cross,
My heart started beating fast,
I had to face the music,
Challenge my mind,

When I thought about it,
For me to cross the river was short,
I ran fast like a springbok,
I felt enlightened afterwards,
But as far I can say,
To cross the river was splendid.

ACTIVITIES(QUESTIONS)

1. According to you, what caused the poet to cross the river?
2. While the poet was crossing the river, he
   felt somehow. List 2 feelings he had.
3. What will you have, when you make bad decisions?
4. I had too many decisions in my head. How?
5. My heart started beating fast.
   a) Give the synonym of fast.
   b) Give the antonym of fast.
6. Face the music.
   a) Explain it.
   b) What part/figure of speech is this?
   c) When and where is the expression used?
7. Why was it very short for the poet to cross the river?
8. The poet used comparison on stanza 3.
   Quote it from the poem.
9. Why was he feeling enlightened?
10. Why was it very splendid to the poet to cross the river?
11. According to your understanding of the poem,
    what can you regard the river with?
12. The poet used apostrophe in the poem. Support this statement.

6

An Anonymous Dad

By: Musa Masombuka

After so much secrets and conspiracy within the family, I noticed that year by year I am introduced to a new father. So it was time for me to take action, but what kind of? The poem came to my mind, an anonymous dad, because I didn't know my real father and the reason why I've been kept away from him for such long time.

Everyday I ask myself a question,
I do not find an answer,
I ask myself about my daddy,
I wonder if I have one,
I have never seen him,
I don't even know his name,
Is this his face,
That I see on the mirror,
When I wake up?

Mom is always there for me,
But her presence is mediocre,
The other half of me is lacking,
For a father figure,
We never had a conversation about him,
I don't know who to blame,
When boys talk about their daddies,
I feel neglected,
I feel like I'm not part of them,

His absence in my life,
Has left me in an empty world,
People are asking whatsoever questions,
Which I can't endure,
I wish you could come back home,
And live the life we always daydreamed,
Daddy I need you in my life,
Please come home,

ACTIVITIES(QUESTIONS)

1. Why did the poet choose the title 'An anonymous dad'?
2. What does the poet mean when he says
   'I don't know who to blame'?
3. Why is he saying that his mom is mediocre?
4. What is the meaning of mediocre?
5. 'His absence has left me in an empty world'.
   a) What figure of speech is this?
   b) Why is he saying so?
6. What kind of questions are whatsoever questions?
7. What is to endure?
8. The poet used imagery in stanza 1, quote
   14 words to support this statement.
9. a) To what does "we" refer to in stanza 2?
   b) To what does "his" in stanza 4, line 1 refer to?
10. The poet used imagery in stanza 3. Quote
    7 words to support this statement.
11. People are asking whatsoever questions.
    -Who are these people?

7

An Idea Came

By: Thabile Sekgobela

An idea came after experiencing that you do not always have to further your studies to enrich your mind and be a role model to others. The idea of writing came to mind and I took it on a high serious note.

An idea came,
When I tried to terminate my future,
The idea was a once in a lifetime,
Which I couldn't let go,
My life was so upside down,
Thought that everybody has turned their back against me,
I thought about everything,
That could change my circus life into reality.

I failed to come up with a solution,
Until one day this idea came in my mind,
I knew it was time to face the world,
It is so splendid to have ideas,
I learned that conclusion of fools is despair,
In life you have to put all your eggs scattered,
Because you never know which one will hatch.

Life has challenges and rewards,
To get the rewards . . .
You have to face everything it throws at you,
Never let go ideas,
They are the key to unlock your own destiny.

ACTIVITIES(QUESTIONS)

1. In your opinion what idea did the poet have?
2. "My life was so upside down." What does he mean?
3. Why is it so splendid to have ideas?
4. What is to be persistent?
5. "Put all eggs scattered"
   a) State whether idiom or proverb.
   b) Explain the expression.
6. Why does the poet say that never let go ideas?
7. Why did the poet want to terminate his future?
8. Give an expression of the following.
   a) My life was complicated and helpless.
9. Explain this expression.
   a) Unlock the door of your own destiny.
   b) Despair is a conclusion of fools.
10. How will the idea be helpful to the poet?

8

Animal Talk

By: Musa Masombuka

Well . . . You know how some other people are. They treat animals unfair and as if they are not alive. It touched me to see a dog being sick to death but it's owner going for a C.T. Scan check-up every 3months. To take along his dog with him was like a heavy burden. So that's when I realised that people don't love and care about animals they just want to use them for their own benefit.

Heads up!
What have we done to be punished?
We came here as beautiful creatures of God.
We were brought here by purpose, we have our voices to be heard,
But how do we look and sound to humans?
Our voices to them are like pieces of trash,

They oblige us to understand their language,
But why can't they understand ours?
Messiah please help us!
We have turned into sacrifices,
We are sold out for commercial purposes,
We don't get what we want.

They pretend to love us while they don't,
We sleep outside during impossible weathers,
We work hard like there are rewards waiting for us,
We can talk but to them we're meaningless,
What is this human talk?
Oh!Our language is neglected,
Us, animals . . . We can talk.

ACTIVITIES(QUESTIONS)

1. In line 1,what is "Heads up!" used for?
2. What is the purpose of the poem?
3. Do you think that it is true that animal language is neglected? Why?
4. The poet blames humans for everything. Why?
5. State 3 things that the poet doesn't like, which humans do to animals.
6. Animals sleep outside during impossible weather.
   a) Give an example of an impossible weather.
   b) Give an example of an animal that sleep outside.
7. "Messiah please help us!" What part of speech is this?
8. "We don't get what we want." Give example.

9

Born This Way

By: Musa Masombuka

Remember I told you that this book is a combination of all sorts of writing. This poem has been adapted from the song of an American pop star Lady GaGa. It sends out a message to people that God doesn't make any mistake. He builds everyone with delicate masterpieces and give him a purpose before He brings him/her to the Earth.

I was brought into the world by purpose,
I should never try to fake myself,
I was born and raised with love,
I never listened to dogs that bark at my world,
You can call it a curse,
Or just call me blessed,
If you can't handle my worst,
You can't get my best,

We are all born superstars,
We both make mistakes and learn from them,
Don't hide yourself in regret,
Just love yourself and you'll be great,
Rejoice your truth,
God ain't done mistakes,
You were born this way.

ACTIVITIES(QUESTIONS)

1. Why should you never fake yourself?
2. Why did the poet not listen to his enemies?
3. Why do you have to not hide yourself in regret?
4. If you can't handle my worst, you can't get my best. Why?
5. We are all born superstars. True or false? Why?
6. Give the message of the poem.

10

Boy Wonder

By: Josiah Molokoane

This poem I dedicated it to a friend of mine who loved attending church and also a hardworker. He had no support when he was at his worst, he worked as a slave. His condition touched me and this poem came up.

He is black and brown,
On top lay of his crown,
Never angry but scowls,
He worked till he was blown,
Cool as the morning mist,
He relaxed was in danger,
He was identified with a kiss,
Yet he shown no anger,
Was he human or devine?
Did he even exist?
Is he still shining bright?
Was he in any opportunist?
Son of a man or not,
He pleased God.

ACTIVITIES(QUESTIONS)

1. Take out 4 words that rhyme together.
2. What race is Wonder?
3. Wonder was God's servant. Quote from the poem to support this.
4. Wonder is hardworker. Quote a phrase from the first 5 lines which proves the statement.
5. Wonder was of the royal family. Quote one word in first three lines which proves the statement.
6. They never wanted Wonder to rest. What if he did?
7. Did Wonder have any wife or girlfriend?
8. Why the poet asks that: 'Was he a human or divine?'
9. This poem is a fiction poem. Quote one word in line ten to support this.
10. What was Wonder doing to earn a living?

11

Complicated

By: Musa Masombuka

My girlfriend started to act different to impress me. But what she never knew was that I loved her unconditionally. My love for her was very deep. But she didn't accept herself. So this poem I wrote to inform her that, she just has to be herself, never try to pretend to be somebody because it complicates our relationship. If she can do so then life would be wonderful.

Love is a feeling,
That binds two hearts together,
Everyone deserve to be loved,
Does it cost too much to be who you are?
I love you the way you are,
Why do you have to make things so complicated,

The way you're acting,
Is like you're somebody else,
And it gets me frustrated,
You're trying to be cool,
You look like a fool to me,

Life is like this:
We fall, we crawl,
We break and take what we get,
And we turn it into honesty,

Promise me,
I'm never gonna find you fake it,
Accept the way you are,
Then life will be wonderful.

ACTIVITIES(QUESTIONS)

1. What is love?
2. Everyone deserves to be loved. True or False?
3. What is the poem talking about?
4. What gets the poet frustrated?
5. To what gender is the poem dedicated?
6. The poet likes his girlfriend keeping it real. Quote from the poem to support this.
7. How is the girl complicating things?
8. How is life to the poet.

12

Cupcakes

By: Musa Masombuka

I came from school and I was hungry. Only to find out that no food was prepared besides the delicious cupcakes. They were baked for the occasion, as I didn't know . . . I thought they were baked to be eaten while there will still be lunch to be prepared. So I ate some, mom came and shouted at me . . . I was ravenous, I couldn't help. So before I left to school, I wrote her this letter.

I am sorry,
I ate the cupcakes that were in the breadbox,
I was ravenous,
And they were scrumptious,
I couldn't help,
They took over my taste buds,
I know you saved them for the occasion,
My tongue was craving for them,
I know you could be angry,
Though I think is you being mischievous,
Please forgive me.

ACTIVITIES(QUESTIONS)

1. Why is the poet sorry?
2. Why did he eat the Cupcakes?
3. What is a breadbox?
4. How were the cupcakes?
5. The cupcakes were baked for what?
6. Why does the poet say that, if the person who baked them could be angry, it'll be because he/she is mischief?
7. Do you think that the baker of the cupcakes is mischief?

13

Death

By: Thabang Tshwane

Death comes in many ways and most hurting is that death doesn't warn or notify. You never know when you gonna love the one you love. I compared it to an unexpected visitor, because it comes so suddenly and unexpectedly.

Death is an unexpected visitor,
An unexpected visitor who brings tears and sadness,
A visitor who spends a little time with you,
But remembered forever.
A visitor who makes happy moments fade,
A visitor who unites families to share the sorrow story,
A visitor who is a sinful creature to leave you in pain,

Death is like a visitor,
Whose last words are captured,
A visitor who says the final goodbye,
A visitor whose decisions are not changed,
An unexpected visitor who is given huge respect,
This visitor is the one who will drain your pockets,
This visitor is only there to remind you one thing . . . .

Life is short and sweet,
Death . . . . An unexpected visitor.

ACTIVITIES(QUESTIONS)

1. To what does the poet compare death with?
2. What figure of speech is "Death is like an unexpected visitor."
3. Why this visitor brings sadness and tears?
4. In your opinion, what happened to this visitor?
5. Is it true that this visitor is there to drain your pockets? How?
6. Write the message of the poem.
7. Explain this expressions.
   a) Life is short and sweet.
   b) sinful creature to leave you in pain.
8. How do you feel about this poem? (give a reason).
9. In your opinion, is death an unexpected visitor?
10. Why?

14

Don't think they know

By: Musa Masombuka

Well you know how greedy people are. They like making conclusions when it comes to the matter of others, they're unable to manage their own but they think they can deal with those of others. And most embarrassing is that they spread rumours that are not true about someone, you will hear them saying that "I am talking from the horse's mouth."

People like to interfere where not necessary,
They seek a way to meddle in the affairs of others,
They like making forward reflections as if they have clues,
A wise person would never fall for what they say,
Don't think they know, even if they say so,
Some like success,
But to others success is a sin,
They like to complicate the life of others,
They know that they would never be the same as them,
Gossiping is what pulls them back,
They like to say that they are talking from the horse's mouth,
While they heard rumours,
Don't think they know,
When they try to threaten you, don't think they know.

ACTIVITIES(QUESTIONS)

1. Why do people like to interfere?
2. Why can't a wise man listen to them?
3. How do they know the affairs of others?
4. Why is success a sin to them?
5. Why they like to complicate other's lives?
6. What is it that pulls them back?
7. Rumour has it. Quote from the poem to support this statement.

15

Education

By: Musa Masombuka

After realising that education plays an important role to everyone. I ask that what will we would've been without education? The root of education is bitter but the fruit is sweet. Why is that? L.O.L ask yourself.

Education who are you?
Education where do you come from?
Why are you so humbled?
What do you worth in everyday life?
Education! Education! Education!

I heard rumours about you,
That you have everyone's life in your palms,
Do you also have mine too?
Education where are your parents?
Why have they abandoned you?
You are a street kid who needs proper care,
But that care is worth our pockets,

Education why are you so tickled pink?
Education why are you so ill-mannered?
If I were you,
I would have to be born again,
Maybe you will change.

ACTIVITIES(QUESTIONS)

1. What figure of speech is the poem as a whole?
2. Do you think that education is humbled?
3. What does education worth?
4. Education has our lives on it's palms, true or false? Why?
5. Why does the poet say:'Education where are are your parents?'
6. Education is a street kid. How?
7. Why is education worth our pockets?
8. Why education is so tickled pink?
9. What is to be tickled pink?
10. Education can be your best friend or your worst nightmare. True or false?
11. Education itself is ill-mannered or is it the people who took care of it who are ill-mannered? How?
12. Give and example of where education is found.
13. If you could meet education, would you be able to hold and poke him? Give a reason to your answer.

16

Falling In Love

By: Mapule Pila

My first day at the beach and also my first date. The moments we had were the greatest, I wished if Summer time stayed longer. So that we spend more time at the beach. I was really thrilled and carried away by the fancy words he tells.

The bright sun and the blue water,
We fight less and love harder,
We watch the stars in the clear skies,
We walk the beach at midnight,
You tell me that I'm the one,
I tell you it's just for fun,
We both say I Love You,
We hold hands for too long,
We tell of a love story,
I was carried away by the fancy words,
You proved yourself that you are the one,
I tell you, you're the king of my heart,
I really fell for you,
Because I Love You!

ACTIVITIES(QUESTIONS)

1. Briefly describe the message of the poem.
2. What are fancy words?
3. What does the poetess mean when she says "You are the king of my heart"?
4. What is the gender of the poetess?
5. What figure of speech is used on "I really fell for you"?
6. What is love?
7. Is love a noun, adverb, article or adjective?
8. Write love as an adjective.
9. This poem is a reality poem, specify whether it is happening indoors or outdoors. Provide a reason.

17

Fatherless me, Motherless I

By: Musa Masombuka

This poem I wrote it after I experienced that there are many abandoned children out there whom think that they are orphans but their parents are still out there. Parents should take full responsibility to their children because they're the reminder of their true love and most precious gifts. Ain't you lucky you have children? There are some parents out there who can't have them. So please love them like you love yourself.

Hello strange parents,
What went wrong about me?',
I was born after love,
But I grew up under hatred,
Mother, how did you feel,
Having me around?
Father, What presentation was I to you?
The world has neglected me,
How could you make me an orphan,
While I'm not?

What broke the love I was born after?
When I look around,
I don't have a shoulder to rely on,
You left me in an impossible position,
Fatherless me, Motherless I.
My dignity has faded,
Because you left me,
I have no brother or sister,
I thought I was a precious gift to you,
But oh! Fatherless me, Motherless I.

ACTIVITIES(QUESTIONS)

1. Why does the poet start by "Hello strange parents"?
2. They poet was born after love, but grew up under hatred. Why?
3. They parents of the poet are no longer in an relationship. Quote from the poem.
4. The parents of the poet are still alive out there. Quote from the poem.
5. The poet was only the baby of his parents. Quote from the poem.
6. The poet thought his parents loved him. Quote from the poem.
7. The poet knows nothing about the relationship of his parents. Quote from the poem.
8. The poet thought that he was alone. Why?
9. Briefly describe the message of the poem.

18

First birthday

By: Musa Masombuka

I was invited to a birthday party of a 1 year old boy. The birthday was special but the boy was frightened and surprised by the crowd, music and all the up and downs because it was for the first time he experienced such thing. We felt like strangers in his own company.

Remember on your first birthday,
We were celebrating your first year,
We were so happy for you,
You ignored us,
Pretended like you have no idea,
You embarrassed us,
You thought that days were the same,
We tried to cheer you up with cakes and drinks,
We tried to play music to make you sing with us,
But what we gave you was a fright,
You never smiled, not even said a word like before,
We felt like strangers in your accompany,
We saw that you were bored with us,
First birthday, first birthday.

ACTIVITIES(QUESTIONS)

1. How old is the person whose birthday is celebrated?
2. They were so happy, but he ignored them. Why?
3. He thought days were the same. Why?
4. They gave him a fright. Why?
5. Why didn't he smile or say a word?
6. Why did people feel like strangers in the accompany of the birthday boy?
7. Do you think that he pretended like he had no idea?

19

He, who saved me

By: Thabang Aphane

God does things amazing and mysterious. No one can compare to his powers and miracles. This poem talks about a blind person whom many has failed to cure but God came to his rescue and opened his eyes to light.

I had eyes but I could not see,
You wouldn't distinguish,
The difference between,
Who was blind and I,
The eyes I had were just useless,
Because there were no sight,
I spoke the language of the blinds,
And even behaved in their manner.

The eyes I had,
Started becoming weight to my shoulders,
The weight I never wanted to carry,
Many wanted to take it off me,
The question was, should I?
No I shouldn't.

He came in my life,
And showed me the purpose of them,
He found me,
And He rescued me from all the blinds.

ACTIVITIES(QUESTIONS)

1. Who is He?
2. Why were the eyes of the poet useless?
3. The poet and the blind person were the same. Why?
4. The poet ended up behaving like a blind. Why?
5. Why did the eyes of the poet become heavy to him?
6. What did 'He' do for the poet?
7. Briefly describe the message of the poem.

20

Home is where the heart belongs

By: Musa Masombuka

Yeah it's true, everyone belongs at a special place of memories called home. No matter how far you may be but your final place is your home. It is your root, sense of belonging, ain't a place like it. Home sweet home.

Home . . .
Such a beautiful place where everyone belongs,
It is a place of memories,
A place where the spirit of a person belongs,
A place which can't be forgotten,
A place which is always there should you suffer.

A place of courage and guidance,
A rose may be separated from its stem but not from its smell,
You may be faraway,

But your heart belongs at your home,
Home, sweet home.

ACTIVITIES(QUESTIONS)

1. Everyone belongs at (a)_____. It is a place of (b)_____.
2. Why this place can't be forgotten?
3. What figure of speech did the poet use in stanza 2, line 3 and 4?
4. 'Home sweet home', why did the poet conclude with this words?
5. Why this place is always there for you?
6. In your opinion, do you think that other people forget this place? Why?
7. Correct the following errors.
   Hume is **sach** a **beatiuful** place **were** everybody belongs. A place which **can** be **fogortten**, a place of **discourage** and **misfortune**. Home, **sour** home.

21

I Am Me

By: Musa Masombuka

This time I send out a message that I am me and that's all I want to be. I will deal with my own problems, my own way and live my own life. So you too be yourself and deal with challenges suitable for you. Don't be someone because you might regret it at the end.

I Am me,
That's all I wanna be,
In this world I was brought alone,
Alone to be myself and follow my dreams,
Dreams that will lead me to success,
Success the mother of good life,
Good life that is everyone's wish,
Wish that has to be fulfilled,
Fulfilled to make us happy,
Happiness that will last forever,
Forever between our hearts,
Heart the image of a person,
Heart that reveals a tortoise in its shell.
Tortoise the shy creature on earth.
I Am me and that's all I wanna be.

ACTIVITIES(QUESTIONS)

1. The poem is an apostrophe. Give a reason
   to support the statement.
2. What are dreams?
3. How is success being described in the poem?
4. 'Forever between our hearts.' what part of speech is this?
5. A heart that reveals a tortoise in its shell.
   -Explain this in your own words.
6. 'I am me and that's all I wanna be." what does
   these words tell you about the poet?

22

I am nobody's fool

By: Lesego Kgwete

Well . . . You already got the message on the title. I am nobody's fool
is a poem written after I experienced that people noticed that I give
them my full attention, so they take me as a fool and I allow them to
do that because deep down I know that I ain't a fool.

I am unwritten,
You can't read my mind,
I'm undefined,
I break tradition,
Everything depends on my hands,
How do people see me like?
When I accomplish everyone's request,
When I listen to melodies of tweeting birds,
When I even listen to animal talk,
I am a fool to everyone,
But only a fool is a successful person,
I exhort politeness and comprehensibility from my heart,
People use me however they like to,
I follow every wind they blow,
What I know is that,
There's a reward waiting for me,
So I let them take me however they like,
What I know is that,
I am nobody's fool.

ACTIVITIES(QUESTIONS)

1. Why does the poet say that he is unwritten?
2. They poet is not lazy, quote from the
   poem to support this statement.
3. People take the poet as a fool. List 2 things
   that will suit him for being a fool.
4. The poet has noticed that people take him as a
   fool. Quote from the poem to support this.
5. Only fools are successful. Why?
6. Why is he saying that he is nobody's fool?

23

I knew you were trouble

By: Musa Masombuka

A friend of me tried to seek a way to know me better so that he can fake me . . . He pretended to care and I had a doubt feeling and that's when I realised that he was no true friend after I heard some whispers on the streets whispering me where I walked past.

I was hungry for love,
I had no one to run to,
I thought of all possible solutions,
I failed to find someone to rescue me,
You were there for me,
You hid my shadow,

Protected my soul,
Kindled your amusement and support to me,
I started to have faith in you,
I felt like the dark cloud,
Was removed upon me,
But I had a sudden doubt feeling,
You stole my pride, my dignity and my image,

You admired me only to fake me
I knew you were trouble when we met,
It's a shame on me now,
How could you patronize me,
After all we've been through?
I found it strange,
For what you were trying to do.

ACTIVITIES(QUESTIONS)

1. How did the poet meet his friend?
2. He never thought he'd find one. Quote from the first stanza to support this.
3. What did this new friend of him do?
4. The poet started feeling secured around his friend. Why?
5. The poet's friend was a true friend. True or false? Why?
6. The poet's friend did something that the poet noticed. What is it?
7. What is to patronize?
8. I knew you were trouble, what does the title tell you about the poet's friend?

24

I Poverty

By: Musa Masombuka

It is a reality poem where I personified poverty. People who suffers from poverty are those who didn't listen to the guidance of their parents. Poverty is brought by poor education, unemployment and high rate of pregnancy.

I am a rude child,
A child who everyone doesn't adore,
I was born by my mother 'pregnancy',
And my father 'unemployment',
Surrounded by shit government,
From the townships is where I originate,
I tour wherever I like to.

But my problem is one,
Wherever I enter,
Trouble is what they see,
Please help me,
Where could I hide?
I am an innocent child,
But to them I am a sinner,
I like visiting where their pockets are empty,
Is that too much to ask?
I poverty, the enemy of everyone.

ACTIVITIES(QUESTIONS)

1. The poet used personification, quote from
   the poem to support this statement.
2. Poverty is a child who everyone hates, why?
3. Name the parents of poverty and state how do they interact.
4. Where does poverty originates?
5. How do people treat poverty?
6. Poverty claims to be innocent, but why is he a sinner?
7. What is it that is needed to chase poverty away?
8. Poverty is not ready for improvement. Quote from stanza 2.

25

I think they are thinking

By: Musa Masombuka

People grow up with respect but they abandon it when they're in the adolescence stage. Many have fallen because of that they thought they knew better than everyone. You find that someone is working well earning millions, but his background is poor. Instead of improving his background, he pleases friends by spending money like peanuts. I think they are thinking.

Look!What has happened to the world of peace and democracy,
Unity is neglected,
Peace is deleted,
Respect has depleted,
Crime is restored from the river mouth,
What has fallen upon us humans?

Why do we like to delay the time of others?
Why do we like to poke quiet bees in a hive?
People where is your dignity?
Where is the respect you had from childhood?
Which visitor has visited your mind?
People why do you like to act like you are opponents?

People why do you like to make yourselves onions in a bunch of lemons?
I think they are thinking.

ACTIVITIES(QUESTIONS)

1. Take out three words that rhyme the same in the poem.
2. Take out a rhetorical question in the poem.
3. What is to poke quiet bees?
4. Crime is abroad. Quote from the poem to support this.
5. According to the poet, people have changed. Quote from the poem to support this statement.
6. People like to delay the time of others. How?
7. The trouble has been addressed on the sestet (first six lines). Briefly describe the problem the poet has addressed.
8. What happened to peace, unity and respect?
9. The poet used antithesis on the last 2 lines, give example.
10. What did the poet conclude with?

26

I'm wide awake

By: Thabile Sekgobela

I'm wide awake is a complimentary poem. I thank myself for would've done such a wonderful thing by revealing my talent. It just came to mind.

I was in the dark sleeping on my dreams,
I was dreaming for so long,
I wrongfully read the stars,
My life was so upside down,
I was made asleep by the lullaby,
But then in my morning shine,
I was born again,
Out of the lion's den,
I am wide awake,
I can now identify the unseen failure,
I am able to see the wrong and rights,
God knew that I tried seeing the bright side,
He gave me a vision to excavate my dreams.

ACTIVITIES(QUESTIONS)

1. Who is the singer who sings the song
   as the same title as the poem?
2. "I wrongfully read the stars". Why?
3. Why was the poet sleeping on his dreams?
4. What figure of speech is 'out of the lion's den'?
5. Why this poet can now identify the wrong and rights?
6. 'I am wide awake'. Explain this expression.
7. Who knew that the poet was looking for the bright side?
8. 'He gave me a vision to excavate my dreams.'Explain how.
9. What type of a poem is this?
10. Summarize the message of the poem.

27

I Priest

By: Musa Masombuka

Crime is abroad, even those whom we put our trust on are those who betray us. The churches and the priests are fighting against crime and evil spirits within us humans so that we become 100% christians and our country become crime-free.

Look! What devils has done,
To my beautiful world,
The evil spirits are roaming all over,
Conspiracy is abroad,
Secrets are hidden between walls,
Why God left this beautiful creature?
After what Jesus did for us,
What else do we need?

We are not secured at night,
Our life is tragic everyday,
What they say to us is that:
"It is not over until God says it's over."
Only to console us,
What did we do?
To deserve sinners?

I priest, know that through my Lord,
I can face defeat,
I priest, know that where devils put a full stop,
I begin a new sentence,
I priest, am a testifier of that.

ACTIVITIES(QUESTIONS)

1. What is a priest?
2. Why do evil spirits fly all over?
3. Why is conspiracy abroad?
4. 'After what Jesus has done for us.' What is the poet trying to emphasis?
5. Why are were not secured at night?
6. What do they say to console us?
7. What is to console?
8. The priest can face defeat, through who?
9. Where devils put a full stop. I begin a new sentence. Explain how.

28

An intoxicated man

By: Josiah Molokoane

This poem I saw it live at the bar. The conversation between the bar lady and the very drunk Robert asking for another bottle of beer. It came to my mind in such that people are really addicted to liquor whereby they almost forget their state of position and manner.

Man oh clumsy man,
Why is it hard for you to stand?
You are physically capable,
Of standing still,
But you walk like you're intensely ill,
What is your name? she asked,
Robert, the white man said,
Of what nature is the act?
Oh baby, you don't understand,
Please enlighten me sir,
I had 1 glass,
Only to have what I see twirl,
Oh my God, you must get home,
I can get there on my own,
Oh! Dear don't get hurt,
Ma'am don't worry about that,

ACTIVITIES(QUESTIONS)

1. Where was Robert?
2. In what state/condition is Robert?
3. It was hard for Robert to stand. Why?
4. Who was Robert speaking to?
5. What race is Robert?
6. Robert is capable of standing still. What will happen if he takes a step?
7. Robert said to the bar lady that he can walk himself home. Can he? Why?
8. Why did Robert drink?
9. What is to twirl?

29

Jai Ho!

By: Musa Masombuka

A poem I wrote after I experienced on the media that a mother has an undying love when it comes to her children. And children exhort that love back to her, it is so exciting!

My mother,
You're my everything,
You're all I ever wanted,
You're the reason why I still breathe,
You're my life,
You're my destiny,
Jai Ho!

Remember the sacrifices you made,
For me to be a human being,
Remember how many edges of knives you held,
For me to feel protected,
Remember those days you arose and hid my shadow,
For me to be where I am today,
To you I salute,
Because Jai Ho! (You're my destiny.).

ACTIVITIES(QUESTIONS)

1. What is the meaning of Jai Ho!?
2. The poet dedicated the poem to someone, who is it?
3. List 3 things that the mother of the poet did.
4. The poet says that:'You're the reason why I still breathe.' why?
5. The poet say that:'You're all I ever
   wanted.' What about his father?
6. How do you feel about this poem? Why?
7. According to you, when did the poet write this poem?

30

Little Girl [explicit]

By: Musa Masombuka

Greedy! Greedy! Greedy! Adolescence is a very dangerous stage to deal with. So if parents doesn't take action by talking to their children about this kind of things, this is what happens.

She thought she was mommy's little girl,
Until one man came to her,
And greed her to sex,
She only knew him by the pronoun 'He'.
He brought her to pain,
With a cock of diseases,

Tears running from her eyes,
Down to her cheeks,
She didn't know what was happening,
She screamed for help,
Help to rescue her from a stranger,
A stranger she thought he loved her,
Poor little girl felt like a dumped piece of trash,
Trash that will never be recycled,

From the moment she knew,
How greedy can leave you in an inappropriate position,
Mommy's little girl was never like before,

ACTIVITIES(QUESTIONS)

1. What happened to the girl?
2. She didn't know the man. Quote a phrase to support this.
3. Why was the girl in pain?
4. Why was she crying?
5. What is a cock?
6. What tells us that the man had STI's?
7. The girl thought one thing about the man, what is it?
8. After having sex, how did the girl feel?
9. What have the girl learnt from the man?
10. The girl was sick, what kind of disease did she have?
11. The girl didn't think that the man was
    sick. Quote from the poem.

31

Love Story

By: Musa Masombuka

Well . . . It is a love story of me and my girl. How simple she brings that love to me. The romantic times we spend together, she really means the world to me. She really is my angel sent from above. Love story, love story, how interesting her love is deep to me.

Where do I begin,
To tell the story of how great love can be?
The sweet story that is older than the sea,
The simple truth about the love she brings to me,
Where do I start?

With her first hello,
She gave a meaning to this empty world of mine,
There will never be another love like this,
Another time to seek love,
She came into my life and made living fine,
She fills my heart with very special things,
With wild imaginations,
She fills my soul with so much love,
Wherever I go,
I am never lonely,
With her along, who could be lonely?

How long does love last?
Can love be measured by hours in a day?
I have no answer now,
I know I will need her,
Until the stars all burn away,
And she will be there.

ACTIVITIES(QUESTIONS)

1. To what gender is the poem dedicated to?
2. 'The sweet story that is older than the sea.' What figure of speech is this?
3. "With her first hello, she gave a meaning to this empty world of mine."
   a) Explain this.
   b) What figure of speech is this?
4. What tells you that these two are really in true love?
5. What does she do to the poet? List 2 things.
6. Why is the poet never lonely?
7. What tells you that these 2 will live happily together forever?
8. 'Can love be measured by hours in a day?'
   -What kind of a question is this?

---⟨⟨◉⟩⟩---

32

Make you feel my love

By: Musa Masombuka

I try to express my feelings to my girl that I could do anything to prove my love for her. I am never scared of a commitment, that's why I am game for any adventure when I am to prove how deep my love is for her.

When days are dark,
When the evening shadows appear.
When you feel like you're alone,
I could offer you a warm embrace,
To make you feel my love.
When your so-called friends have forgotten you.
And you need a shoulder to cry on,
I could hold you for a million years,
To make you feel my love.

When the world has turned into a stranger to you,
Know that I am always here for you,
I know it is strange to be supportive so much,
But I will never do you wrong,
I have known it from the moment that we met,
There's no doubt in my heart where you belong,
There is nothing I couldn't do,
I could even go to the end of the Earth for you,
To make you feel my love.

---⟨⟨◉⟩⟩---

ACTIVITIES(QUESTIONS)

1. Briefly describe what is happening in the poem.
2. When days are dark. How?
3. What is the poet determined to do, to make her feel his love?
4. What are "So-called friends"?
5. Why is it so strange to be so much supportive these days?
6. There is no doubt in my heart where
   you belong. Briefly describe.
7. In stanza 2, the poet tells us that he is ready to do everything
   for her. Quote 6 words to support this statement.
8. The poet says that he can go to the ends
   of the Earth for her. Can he? Why?

33

Making my moves

By: Thabile Sekgobela

Making my moves, this poem goes hand in glove with I'm wide awake. I still compliment myself though on this one I am addressing that ever since I took out my writing talent I had many enemies. I pretended not to see that they hate me but I knew they were not happy for me when I made my move.

Oh tears of joy,
Thinking about something, it is very so dark,
Making melodies,
Oh making my moves,
Like I never did before,

Found that everyone hates me,
Except myself,
Oh moves that makes me,
Believe in this world,
Started walking,
Telling good stories,
Pretending that life is Ok,
So slender,
So bright,

Oh mirror, mirror,
Who is the best of them all?
My aim was to make my move,
And earn a living.

ACTIVITIES(QUESTIONS)

1. What exactly do you understand about the poem?
2. Why was the poet making his moves?
3. What tells you that the poet was lost?
4. When the poet started making his moves, what did he discover?
5. 'So slender, so bright.' what does these words tell you about the moves of the poet?
6. Why was the poet telling good stories?
7. What is the vocation of the mirror in the poem?

34

My first dice

By: Thabile Sekgobela

On this poem I am alerting people to think first before they make up their mind. I did things that I'd never tell, they are so dangerous and untold. That's why when I sat down and listened to myself, the poem came to mind.

I never played an important role in my life,
I turned good things into bad,
I never learned from my mistakes,
When everybody told me,
It felt like life came to an end,

I never relinquish on something,
But when I played my first dice,
I did give up so badly,
It took many days and months,
To make up my mind,
For the first day I realised that,
You have to play nice on your first dice.

When the dice rolls it tells something,
It tell you that if you're thinking straight,
You will walk on the good lane,
When playing the first dice.

ACTIVITIES(QUESTIONS)

1. What did the poet compare the dice with?
2. Did he play an important role in his life? Why?
3. What happened to the words he got from others?
4. The poet was confident in his life. Give
   a reason to support this.
5. Why do you have to play your first dice nicely?
6. What is to make up your mind?
7. What will the dice tell you?
8. What have you learned from the poem?

35

People talk

By: Thabang Tshwane

One thing common to everyone is gossiping. There ain't a way whereby you do something then they keep quiet. There will always be comments and rumours. So in this poem you must learn to ignore.

In this world,
You have to be your own boss,
Your performance is your own responsibility,
But there's one thing in common,
People talk,
They masquerade to be courageous,
But they move under your feet,

As a person you have to ignore,
Gossiping will not brighten up your day,
The busy bodies are abroad,
You do good or bad things,
People talk,
Let them talk because there's no reward,
In their minds, hearts, day and night,
They are always talking.

They try to motivate,
While they paint pictures of you,
You're successful or poor,
You're ugly or beautiful,
You respect or abhor,
People always talk.

ACTIVITIES(QUESTIONS)

1. How can you be your own boss?
2. What is the common thing in the poem?
3. What is to masquerade?
4. Why do they masquerade to be courageous?
5. What are busy bodies?
6. What does these people benefit?
7. What is to paint pictures about someone?
8. What is it that won't brighten up your day?
9. Why do you have to ignore?
10. People are always talking. Quote from stanza 2 to support this statement.

36

Phrases blown by wind

By: Musa Masombuka

It is a life journey where many have fallen because they never listened, they blew courage away. So they have to suffer the consequences.

Who should be blamed when a leaf falls from a tree?
Is it the wind that blew it away,
Or is it the tree that let it go?
Or is it the leaf who grew tired holding on,
Courage is blown away everyday,
Support is lame to them,
Guidance is a cliche to them,
Life unfolds a lot of misunderstandings,
Everyday, Every moment,
It is up to us to solve it,
Leave it,
Or live with it.

ACTIVITIES(QUESTIONS)

1. What is the poet comparing a tree with?
2. What causes the leaf fall from a tree? List 2 things.
3. The poet used apostrophe in the poem. Why and how?
4. Life unfolds what?
5. What is it that we have to do to succeed in life?
6. What are those misunderstandings?
7. What causes people not to succeed in life?

37

Poetry

By: Musa Masombuka

I am just praising poetry, it plays a role in our everyday life and people are not aware of that. Poetry in music, poetry in movies, poetry in writings. It is time for them to know how important poetry is.

Poetry is education,
Education is wisdom,
Poets unite poetry,
In the poetic pot,
Cooking inspiration,

Poetry hides from the words it speaks,
Poetry is the music of entertainment,
Poetry is love from Africans,
Poetry the paragon of sweet love and bad pain,

Poetry the art of language,
Poetry that gathers feelings,
Poetry that speaks.

ACTIVITIES(QUESTIONS)

1. What is poetry?
2. What do you find in poetry? List 2 things.
3. Who unites poetry?
4. Poetry hides from the words it speaks. Give example.
5. Poetry the music of entertainment.
   What figure of speech is this?
6. The paragon of sweet love and bad pain.
   -Explain the statement.
7. How is poetry regarded to language?
8. What does poetry gather?

38

Shattered Heart

By: Musa Masombuka

A girl whom I though she was my one and only, dumps me unexpected. I thought we had something between the wals, but she said she would like to move on. It broke my heart to know that I failed her.

Babe, when you left I lost the part of me,
It is still so hard for me to believe,
Can you please come back?
You promised not to break my heart,
I gave you my heart as fragile as it is,

You told me that in the case of emergency,
You won't break it you'll call me,
What have I done,
That made you to shatter my heart?
I try to keep things together,
But they keep falling apart,
Because the other half of me is missing,
My love for you never stopped.

My heart is puzzled,
Please come back, I need you,
From the bottom of my shattered heart,
I love you.

ACTIVITIES(QUESTIONS)

1. Who shattered the heart of the poet?
2. What kind of a heart is a shattered heart?
3. The poet lost the part of him, why?
4. I gave you my fragile heart.
   a) What figure of speech is this?
   b) The poet's heart needs proper care, quote one word from the sentence.
   c) Give the antonym of fragile.
5. In the case of emergency.
   a) Which emergency?
   b) Why did she has to call him?
6. The poet tries to keep things together.
   a) How?
   b) What causes them to fall apart?
7. What word from the poem tells you that the heart of the poet is in pieces?
8. Quote a phrase from the poem which tells us that the poet still loves his girl.
9. The poet used imagery on the poem as a whole.
   a) Quote one word from the poem that is used as a pun.
   b) What is the duty of the word in the poem?
   c) What is the duty of the word scientifically?

39

SIM Card

By: Musa Masombuka

Well . . . This one I wrote it deliberately. I want to see if people can see the role played by the small card with big connections.

I am a small thing,
My values are of an enormous thing,
Without me a cellphone is nothing,
Like planet without life,
I am a life saver,

I rescue people in paradise,
I bring connectivity to life,
I am a human's need,
A cellphone is my friend,
I SIM card, a small card with big connectivity.

ACTIVITIES(QUESTIONS)

1. What does SIM stands for?
2. Name any 2 sim cards service providers you know.
3. A cellphone without me is nothing. True or false?
4. What does a SIM card do for people?
5. Why do you think a sim card is a need to humans?
6. Prove that a sim card and a cellphone interact.

40

Someone in my lane

By: Thabile Sekgobela

Someone in my lane is a poem I wrote after a friend of mine turned into an enemy after hearing about my succession. Instead of congratulating me, he said that it is not the first time people write books. He always held that I don't succeed in life and school. That's how the poem originated.

Growing up for me,
I never relinquished on something,
I knew there was something to think of,
To avoid someone in my lane,
He followed my road wherever I went,
I wish he could leave me in peace,
He was a dark cloud in front of my destiny,
I did things to stop him but he kept coming,
Those who knew what I was going through, said: "You have to unlock the door of your own dreams."
Someone in my lane,
I thought he admired my footsteps to follow,
But oh!He was to ruin my journey,
He smiled when I looked at him,
Pretending to care,
Someone in my lane.

ACTIVITIES(QUESTIONS)

1. What is:
   a) A lane
   b) To relinquish
   c) Escort.
2. Someone in the poet's lane. What was he doing?
3. The poet tried to stop him but he followed him. Why?
4. The poet's heavy burden pretended to care. Why?
5. Those who knew what the poet was going through, told him something. What did they say?
6. Why was he stopping the poet from reaching his destiny?
7. Give a short message of the poem.

41

Song of animals

By: Musa Masombuka

It is an imagery poem whereby I am imagining the time they say that animals once dulled the world. I bring it back to sense to believe that they once did rule the world.

Once in a time,
Where animals ruled the world,
They had a ceremony,
On a summer's day,
They sang a song,
Chanting big animals,
Tweeting birds,
Roaring echo animals,
Rabbits & Peacocks with their beauty,
A happy song they sung:

'Moo, moo, meeh meeh,
Miaow, miaow, click clack,
Roar roar, quack quack,'
They sung happily,
With the shining sun,
Scattered clouds,
Cool breeze,
And irresistible shadows of the boabab tree,
The animals had a happy song.

ACTIVITIES(QUESTIONS)

1. List 3 things (surroundings) where the ceremony was happening.
2. 'Chanting big animals.' Give example of a chanting animal.
3. 'Roaring big animals.' Give example of a roaring animal.
4. Give the name of the animals with the following sounds.
   a) Moo.
   b) Meeh.
   c) Miaow.
   d) Click clack.
   e) Roar.
   f) Quack.

42

Started from the bottom

By: Lesego Kgwete and poets

We've put our minds together to come up with this poem. When we told people that we are working on a poetry book, they were like "Oh! Many has failed. How you prosper?." So this time we did it. Can we get their negative comments again?

Things are so much easy to start,
When we started our career,
People had negative comments,
'You will never succeed'
We never listened to what they said,
Because we knew we could make it,
People thought that only famous people do better,
What they never knew is that they all started like us,
We faced defeat and turned it into victory,
We started from the bottom now we're here.
Can we hear a SHOUTOUT from our foes?
Yeah, it's us you undermined,
Now we are on our fast lane,
Because we started from the bottom going to the top.

ACTIVITIES(QUESTIONS)

1. All things start from the bottom. True or false?Give a reason to support your answer.
2. When the career of the poets started, how did people react?
3. Why didn't they listen to them?
4. What is it that people thought?
5. What is it that people never knew?
6. The team faced defeat and turned it into victory. Which defeat?
7. The team is famous now. What did they do?
8. What would have happened if they started from the top?
9. Why does the team want to hear a SHOUTOUT from its enemies?
10. The team is now on the rollercoaster of joy. What 2 words tells us that?

43

Summer Spring

By: Musa Masombuka

Two seasons put together. Yes, they bring best results when they react. We plant and harvest. Enjoy the fruits and vegetables in Summer under the tree shadow, sharing laughter and good stories. There is so much fun in this poem.

I like to see trees blossom,
I love to see the green pastures,
The beauty of nature,
Greening like the summer pastures,
I like to see the blue waters,
Swimming in the shining sun,
Summer the paragon of harvest,

The cool breeze in the dawn,
Sitting around the firewood,
Enjoying pot flakes and laughter,
In Summer sitting under the shadow,
Enjoy the mouth-watering taste,
Of summer fruits from vines and orchards,
The cold sweet taste of pears,
Like the berries will blacken on your tongue and fingers,

I like to see all sorts of shorts,
All sorts of skirts in the pool,
On the blistering sun,
In the summer fling,
Oh!December.

ACTIVITIES(QUESTIONS)

1. List 5 things that the poet loves about Spring in stanza 1.
2. How is Summer being described in the poem?
3. State whether Summer or Spring.
   a) The cool breeze in the dawn.
   b) Mouth-watering taste of fruits.
4. What are vines?
5. In stanza 2, list 5 things that the poet loves about Summer.
6. Like berries will blacken on your tongue.
   a) What figure of speech is this?
   b) Briefly explain it.
7. What kind of the sun is the blistering sun?
8. Why does the poet conclude with 'Oh December'?

44

Talk A Good Game [explicit]

By: Musa Masombuka

Well . . . . This time boys are troublemakers. They fool girls by the phrase 'I love you' while they don't mean it. After the fun of love, the boy finds himself in a situation of being a father to be. Then he run away from the poor girl, with a heavy burden.

Boys talk a good game,
They are the professors of lying,
They flog a dead horse,
Boys are always right,
Nothing to them is impossible,
Their good game has no reward,
But a heavy burden of course,
With 2 eggs, 1 sausage and a little bit of milk,
They fill a girl's tummy for 9months,
After they escape,
They avoid the music they were were playing,
Good boys are always voted "Mr. Right"
Bad boys likes fun but they are "Mr. Wrong".
So which ones do you choose girls?

ACTIVITIES(QUESTIONS)

1. What is a good game?
2. Boys like lying. Quote from the poem to support this statement.
3. What makes them always right?
4. Why everything to them is possible?
5. What is to flog a dead horse?
6. Why does this good game leave a heavy burden?
7. The following sentence contains hidden
   things, please reveal them.
   -With 2 eggs, 1 sausage and little bit of milk.
   a) What are?:
      i) 2 eggs
      ii) 1 sausage,
      iii) Little bit of milk.
8. What fills the girl's tummy for nine months?
9. Why good boys are Mr. Rights?
10. Bad boys are 'Mr. Wrong'. Why?

45

Teasing

By: Thabile Sekgobela

Teasing, I wrote it after I experienced it frequently. These bullies they bully you by teasing and expect you to whine and then they fight you. So it affected my badly whereby I even wrote this poem alerting people that if someone bullies you, try to ignore and avoid him.

Discrimination,
It's the only thing that black people like,
Treating and teasing,
It's their profession,
It is what makes them feel powered,
Moving their muscles,
Is when they think of being cruel,

Making fun of you,
Is when they discriminate you from the odds,
Fighting one another,
Is when you make them rave and curse,
You have to take it to your heels,
Because when they catch you,
You will weep,
When you have lost your nerve,
Try to avoid them,

When you tell them to backoff,
They will not relinquish on you,
Because you are their target,
When you give them expensive things,
Is when they masquerade to be friendly,
Acting like you know them,
They tease you.

ACTIVITIES(QUESTIONS)

1. a) What offensive language has been used here?
   b) Which group of people is offended?
2. What is it that makes them feel powered?
3. What do they think of when they move their muscles?
4. Take it to your heels.
   -Explain this idiom.
5. What is teasing used as in the poem?
6. Why do you have to avoid them when you lost your nerve?
7. What does they do when you tell them to backoff?
8. What do you have to do, so that they leave you in peace?
9. This group of people you must not play
   jumpy around them, Why?
10. In your opinion, do you think that blacks like to tease?Why?
11. Discriminate you from the odds,
    a) How?
    b) Who are the odds?
12. When you call the shots, do you think they will smile at you?

46

Technology

By: Musa Masombuka

I distinguish the times before and after technology. It brought improvement, made life easier but its side effects are that it is a big spencer and it ruins the youth of today.

What went wrong?
Life was much easier without technology.
Back then when rocks were soft,
When animals once ruled the world,
People were strong and tough,
Because they did everything for themselves,
But Oh! Improvement ruined everything.

Technology was introduced,
Life became easier but difficult,
Our youth are weak,
Everything is all about technology,
It helps a lot,
But ruining our lives meantime,
Electronics are what does everything in the present life,

Life was much easier
When Blackberry and Apple were just fruits.
Technology is a big spender,
Technology is a monster.

ACTIVITIES(QUESTIONS)

1. Life was much easier without technology.
   True or false? Give a reason.
2. Why people were strong and tough before?
3. Why did the improvement ruin everything?
4. Our youth are weak. Give example to prove this statement.
5. Electronics does everything. Give 2 example of electronics.
6. What are Blackberry and Apple?
7. Why technology is a big spender?
8. What is technology?

47

The cold glass

By: Musa Masombuka

*Well . . . The cold glass, I was at work and a pretty girl passed by,
she stopped and said 'hello'. Between I and her there was a magnetic
force attracting each of us. But we couldn't attract because of the
repulsive force caused by the glass.*

I was in a building surrounded by glass,
I saw my one and only passing by,
She stopped and gazed at me,
Because she fell for me,
I tried to reach her hand, but I couldn't,
The glass was separating the two of us.

In the house I was forbidden to go out,
So with the hand of mine and her's on the cold glass,
And a pocket full of soul,
There's no place she went,
She knew I was trying to pull her through,
She just had to remain strong,
Because I never wanted to lose her,
The vacancy inside of my heart was with her.

ACTIVITIES(QUESTIONS)

1. How is the setting of the poem?
2. Why the poet was unable to see his one and only physically?
3. What separated them?
4. A pocket full of soul.
   a) What part of speech is this?
   b) What does it mean?
5. Why didn't he want to lose her?
6. Why did she had to be strong?
7. According to you, was there any hole on the glass? (refer to stanza 2)
8. According to you, where was the poet?
9. What gender is the poet?
10. What type of a poem is this?
    a) Lyric,
    b) Sonnet,
    c) Apostrophe.

48

The day before I was born

By: Musa Masombuka

I am regretting my born because ever since I was born, whatever happens I am the blame. I wish if only the things where the other way round.

It was on the 31st of March 1998,
On a beautiful black Tuesday,
Everyone was impatient,
To see the gift to be brought in the world,
It it so exciting to come to the world,
But so sadly to be alone in the future,
They thought I'd be a gift to them.

Their minds ran opposite directions,
Why am I such a heavy burden to my parents?
They thought I could bring good things,
But what they never knew is that . . .
They gave me a wrong name MUSA.
Mercy Unity Support Abandoned,
I have turned into a stranger to my parents,

They thought they brought an angel,
But then I embarrassed them,
I am a beautiful sinner,
I wish I could turn back the clock,
And be born again,
Maybe I'd be from the lion's den,
The day before I was born . . . .

ACTIVITIES(QUESTIONS)

1. What wrong name did they give to the poet?
2. What does the poet compare his name with?
3. On what day, month and year was the poet born?
4. What is Musa in english?
5. Why is it so sadly to be alone in the future at the end?
6. What is to be impatient?
7. Their minds ran opposite directions.
    a) What part of speech is this?
    b) What does it mean?
8. Why did he turn into a stranger to his parents?
9. Born out of the lion's den.
    a) What does it mean?
    b) Is it simile or metaphor? Why?
10. What is a beautiful sinner?
11. Give an example of a weekday with it's colour. e.g. Blue Monday.

49

The day before tomorrow

By: Thabile Sekgobela

This one is just a happy non-fictional poem. The way people party, enjoy days and prepare ceremonies day-by-day it excites me because they're doing it like they're never promised tomorrow and that's how life should be.

It was on a summer day,
A day that everyone enjoyed,
A day full of happiness and laughter,
The busiest day of them all,
Twitters had followers,
Birds were also tweeting on the streets,

It was a day of joy,
Everyone's wish was fulfilled,
All negative things were put aside,
It was a day of positivity and creativity,
Who knew how tomorrow will be like?

Who knew what tomorrow held?
Will it be the same as this day?
What if tomorrow never came?
What if it was the last jubilation moment?
The day before tomorrow . . .
It will never be same again.

ACTIVITIES(QUESTIONS)

1. Give an example of the day before tomorrow.
2. How was this day?
3. What is the meaning of 'jubilant'?
4. Why did the poet ask that 'what if tomorrow never came'?
5. Why all negative things were put aside?
6. What is the purpose of the poem?
7. What do you think was happening on this day?
8. This day was also special to birds. Quote from the poem to support this.
9. The poet used imagery in stanza 2, line 2. Quote from the poem.

50

The one that got away

By: Lesego Kgwete

I wrote this poem after my girlfriend left me. I was excruiciated, said, angry and confused at the same time. I didn't know what to do. This poem just came into my mind and I bled my pen to it.

Remember at high school when we first met,
We fell inlove and it was great,
Talked about the future like we had a clue,
Never planned that one day,
I'd lose you,

In another life I could be your man again,
We kept full of promises,
Us against the world,
In another life, I could make you stay,
So I don't have to say those words,
The one that got away,
Maybe in another life we will meet again.

ACTIVITIES(QUESTIONS)

1. Where did Lesego meet his lover?
2. They talked about the future like they had a clue. How?
3. What is it that they didn't plan?
4. What happened to Lesego's lover?
5. In another life.
   -Explain this expression.
6. The one who got away, who?
7. What promises did they have?

51

Time

By: Thabile Sekgobela

Time . . . ! Yep, I try to warn you that you must waste time for good things. Day-by-day everything controlled by Time . . . ! So let's make ourselves useful by using time for good things that will outcome with best results for all of us.

Is it time that we waste speaking,
Time we waste thinking,
Time that we look at,
Time that control us,
Time that we waste making our wish,
Time that we use to shine our dreams,
Time that we waste to lie to good people,
Instead we waste time for nothing.

We don't know what will happen tomorrow,
Are we even promised tomorrow?
We waste time doing things that won't help us,
We do wrong things that no one will forget,
We say nothing,
We do nothing,
We end up being nothing,
Let's wake up South Africa,
Time is for everything,

If we think we can do many things,
Time helps us everyday,
Let us use it for good things.

ACTIVITIES(QUESTIONS)

1. What is that the poet is addressing?
2. List 2 extravagant things that we do with time.
3. List 2 useful things we do by time.
4. We do nothing, we say nothing, we be nothing.
   -Explain this idiotic expression.
5. Time is for everything. How?
6. What is the poet's conclusion?
7. Time that we look at it, give example.

52

To my father II

By: Musa Masombuka

This time I blame myself for the cause of the death of my father. I think he had suffered from a depression thinking about me, where am I? Am I well taken care of? etc. On the other side, I am thinking that maybe he rejected me because making me was never his intention.

Maybe you died 'cos everybody,
Asked me where you at,
But it's like each moment,
We just miss each other,
I got your friends weeping and,
Told me you went 6 feet under,
They said that you said you took a break,
Maybe it was 'cos I blamed thee,
For everything that was my mistakes,
I needed to grow,
And I needed to know,
There are some things inside of me,
That I needed to show,
You told me you'd come back when I need you,
You said it so sweetly, I believed you,

Now I wonder that,
When I was born,
Did I chase that glitz, glamour, money, fame and power?
Because if it was like that,
I would forever regret my birth,
You left me in an impossible possition,
Because you died for no sake,
Why didn't you live with me,
The life you always daydreamed,
Daddy please come back home,

I wish that if only memories could build a stairway,
And tears build a lane,
I would have travelled to Heaven
And bring you home,
Just to be with you.
Because I miss you.
From your puzzled son:Musa.

ACTIVITIES(QUESTIONS)

1. The poet assumes one main problem which led to his father's death. What is it?
2. The poet didn't expect that his father could leave him so soon. Quote a phrase in line 3-4 to support the statement.
3. What other thing does the poet assume could've led to his father's death?
4. Why does the poet wonder such things in stanza 2?
5. What is the poet's wish?
6. The poet's father didn't live together with the poet. Quote from the poem to support this.(Stanza 2).
7. Briefly give the message of the poem in no more than 10 lines.

53

To my Father

By: Musa Masombuka

This time I am apologizing for all the wrongs I done to my father. And I miss him a lot. I wish only time was reversible, I would've reversed it to be with him and know him better.

It's been years daddy,
I really really miss you,
I never got a chance to say the final goodbye,
Mommy says you're safe now,
In a beautiful place called Heaven,
The house is quiet without you,

I miss the way you used to tickle me,
I miss your night stories,
You were the greatest daddy,
I am thinking my younger years,
The days we spent together,
The good times and moments we had,

Precious moments than the sun,
Daddy I miss you in my life,
You will always have a place in my heart,
I sleep with the door open, the light on,
For in case you come and kiss me goodnight.
I miss you daddy.

ACTIVITIES(QUESTIONS)

1. What happened to the poet's dad?
2. The poet didn't attend his father's funeral. Quote from stanza 1 to support the statement.
3. The poet misses 2 things about his dad. Name them.
4. The poet used imagery on the last stanza, give example.
5. The house is quiet without his daddy. Why?
6. Precious moments than the sun. What figure of speech is this?

54

A Toxic Lover

By: Musa Masombuka

My girlfriend fools me by playing with love, making forward reflections of a happy ever couple while on the other side she was cheating with my best friend, she thought I'd never find out but I did.

On the first page of our story,
Our future seemed so bright,
We planned everything like we had a clue,
It soon turned out so evil,
After I have realised that,
The grass was green on the other side,
In all the things we've been through,
I thought we had something between the walls,
But that was only my opinion,
You have caused an incurable pain in my heart.

I remember the first day we met,
We said that we will be forever,
You were so kind,
I don't know what came into you,
You promised to take proper care of my fragile heart,
You shivered and it fell,
We were a hand in glove,
Thought that we'd never separate,
But you decided to be a glove,
And separate with my hand.

You are a toxic someone,
You are an imp,
You have became a stranger to me,
You turned into a hiccough on my throat,
You proved thyself that you're toxic,
I don't think I could ever trust you again.

ACTIVITIES(QUESTIONS)

1. Explain this expression.
   -On the first page of our story.
2. We planned everything like we had a clue means:
   a) They planned on a paper using glue.
   b) They planned everything like they knew what will happen.
   c) They planned everything because they loved each other.
3. What does the poet mean when he says
   "You shivered and it fell?"
4. State true or false, then provide a reason.
   -A toxic lover is someone who is kind and loving.
5. "A hand in glove",state whether idiom or proverb.
6. Why this lover has turned into a stranger to him?
7. "You have turned into a hiccough on my
   throat", what figure of speech is this?
8. What is a toxic lover?(consider toxic).
9. Write the following as contractions.
   (i) You have.
   (ii) I will.
   (iii) Do not.
   (iv) I would.
   (v) Will not.
10. What is an imp?
11. "Grass was green on the other side.", explain how.
12. Give the message of the poem.

55

True Beauty Lies In The Heart

By: Thabile Sekgobela

It is true! I don't have to further explain it. Someone might be beautiful from the face but oooops she is so vicious. So you must be meticulous, don't be fooled by the pretty face and slippery tongue.

True beauty is not the appearance of someone.
True beauty is never about the way you do things,
True beauty lies in the heart of a person,
True beauty is in the courteousness of a heart,
A person can be beautiful from the face,

The heart always tells everything about you,
True love and trust makes a good heart,
Believe and faith makes a courageous shadow,
Confidence and pride is what brightens up your day,
Patience is a guideline to joyride,

True love shows itself,
You can not tell love,
You can only feel love,
The fact remains,
True beauty lies in the heart.

ACTIVITIES(QUESTIONS)

1. State two examples of alliteration formula in the poem.
2. What is the meaning of the noun "courteousness"?
3. From the phrase below, state the following.
   -True beauty lies in the heart.
   a. Article.
   b. Conjunction.
   c. Noun.
   d. Object.
   e. Adjective.
   f. Verb.
4. What does the heart tells?
5. According to the poet, what brightens up your day?
6. How is patience described in the poem?
7. What is the fact in the poem?
8. You can't see love, you van feel love. True or False?
9. What is love?

56

True Heroism Lies Within You

By: Musa Masombuka

Yes, be your own hero, your own role model. Have that eager to be something useful in life. Believe in yourself because you are the steering wheel of your own life.

Everybody is born with a talent,
Everybody is born for himself,
Everybody is a born hero,
This can only be there if you believe in thyself.
Trust yourself that you can do it,
Accept whatever comes the way,
Do not admire someone for pleasure,
Admire someone's footsteps to follow,
Find what is hidden within you and let it out.
The only way to success is in your mind.

Live your life with arms wide open,
Be your own hero,
Run your line however you like to,
True heroism lies within you,
Feel the rain on your skin,
No one else can feel it for you,
Only you can let it,
No one else could speak your mind,
Everyday is where your new book begins,
The rest is still unwritten.

ACTIVITIES(QUESTIONS)

1. Do you think that the title of the poem is true? Why?
2. Quote 2 sentences that tells that 'never like someone for good.'
3. Feel the rain on your skin. Explain this.
4. Why does the poet say that everyday is where your new book begins?
5. Why does the poet say that the rest of your book is still unwritten?
6. How can you be your own hero?
7. No one else could speak your mind. Why?
8. Everyone is born for himself. Why?
9. Give the message of the poem.
10. What kind of a poem is this?
    a) A poem that alerts.
    b) A happy poem.
    c) A sad and sorrow poem.

57

Unfaithful Me

By: Musa Masombuka

*I regret the time I crossed my girl. When I remember that I promised
to be her one and only then I failed to keep the promise, the poem
came through my mind.*

My love, I loved you from the place,
Please forgive me,
I promised to be your shadow,
Oh! Unfaithful me,
I promised you that I'll be yours forever.

I know the feeling when I look at you,
It is a feeling I can't express by words,
From the bottom of my heart,
I hope that you could stay,
So that I can explain,
Without you in my life,
I know it won't be the same,

I don't wanna lose you,
In my heart is where you belong,
I broke your trust I know,
Please try to find the inner you,
And forgive me.

ACTIVITIES(QUESTIONS)

1. What is the purpose of the poem?
2. What has the poet done?
3. What promise did the poet make to his lover?
4. The poet knows that what he has done is wrong. Quote 2 words to support this statement.
5. Quote the sentence that shows us that the poet is also sorry.
6. The poet wants to fix things, quote from the poem to support this statement.
7. What have you learned from the poem?

58

Upside Down Room

By: Musa Masombuka

*I compare life to an upside down room, whereby we get abstracted
by lot of influences, challenges and less solutions. In life you must
know what you want and then know what you are going to do to
achieve that.*

The complicated room ever,
The room that differs from all other rooms,
Everything in this room is upside down,
When I look at the mirror,
I see an upside down me,
I can't do anything in this room,
Besides sleeping.

When I sleep I see circulating challenges,
Challenges with different rewards,
I am unable to choose an option,
Because my mind is upside down too,

When I try to drink water,
With an upside down jug,
The water just spills at me,
I walk upside down,
I think upside down,
Truly life is an upside down room.

ACTIVITIES(QUESTIONS)

1. What is happening in this room?
2. The room is complicated. Why?
3. Why can't the poet do something?
4. What does the poet see when he is sleeping in this room?
5. When I drink water with an upside jug, the water spills at me.
    a) Why always water spills at him?
    b) Explain the expression above in simple english.
6. My mind was upside down. Meaning?
7. Briefly describe the message of the poem.

59

What can a brother do for you?

By: Josiah Molokoane

Most brothers uses their friends, instead of mutualising they parasite on them. This poem came to my mind after realising that people uses their friends when they have them but blames for walking away after discovering that they are being used. I mean where is the love?

He can help you get what you need,
What is a true friend to you,
Is he your wallet in a shebeen,
Do you thank your friend when he's honest?
Does he help you when you are at the kowest?
Does brotherly love exist in your relationship,
Is it an affiliation or real friendship?
Is he forever loyal,
Do you trust him,
Do you show him what you feel,
Does he portray to you what is real,
In me he has a friend,
A brother till end.

ACTIVITIES(QUESTIONS)

1. What can a brother do for you?
2. Briefly describe a true friend.
3. What do people take a friend as? (Refer to line 3 to 4).
4. What is brotherly love?
5. Give one word of . . . (Refer to line 7 to 12).
   a) A connection with an organisation etc.
   b) The state of being friends.
   c) For all time.
   d) Faithful (synonym).
   e) To act the part of . . .
6. Give a suitable title of the poem.
7. Give the message of the poem.

60

When you know, you know

By: Musa Masombuka

Don't let them tell you any difference, you know yourself better than anyone. Don't hide the truth because it has its own way of revealing itself. So let them know you before they start judging you.

The truth has the way of revealing itself,
False is what surrounds and delays us,
Opinions are easily changed,
You can fool everybody,
But you can't fool yourself,
You can do things you'd regret,
You can't forget them,

The truth will always,
Set you free from everything,
It is hard to argue with the facts,
To argue with them,
Is when you want to spin in the cycle of tears,
Just let everyone say anything about you,
Because you know your life than others,
As a person you have to be a dreamer,
Don't let rumours fade your luck,
Be focused because when you know, you know.

ACTIVITIES(QUESTIONS)

1. Can you hide from the truth?
2. What is it that delays us?
3. Why opinions are easily changed?
4. Why can't you fool yourself?
5. Why is it hard to argue with the facts?
6. What is it that you must not let it ruin your life?
7. You can do things you'd regret, but you can't forget. Give example.
8. Give the message of the poem.
9. To spin in the cycle of tears. How?

61

Which door?

By: Thabang Aphane

This is what happens to the youth of today. Whereby they become
abstracted by lot of decisions but less solutions. They fail to choose
because they don't know what each adventure holds.

There are many doors,
But I can only open one,
Only if I knew,
What each door holds for me,
For, I can open one,
Each door holds changes,
Good or bad, that's a mystery,
Wrong choice and my life is history,

Each door is an adventure,
A long journey where many have fallen,
Should I open or rethink?
But what if time is wasted?
May I open this, or that one?
What if it has wrong decisions,
Which door, which door?
If I open one and find that it has an evil adventure,
My life will sink,
Which door shall I open?

ACTIVITIES(QUESTIONS)

1. What does each door holds?
2. What if the poet opens the wrong door?
3. Why many have fallen while on the adventure?
4. The poet is in doubt of opening the door, Why?
5. What will happen if he re-thinks?
6. To what are the doors compared to?
7. What rhetorical question is in the poem?
8. Briefly describe the message of the poem.

62

Who is Mapule Pila?

By: Mapule Pila

This time I give my fans a chance to know me better in a short description of a poem. I felt like telling my fans who really am I, so the poem says it all.

Mapule is a girl,
A girl with love and respect,
A girl who doesn't doubt herself,
A girl who pretends to be happy while she's not.
An exquisite and inquisitive girl.
A girl with big dreams and mission.

A girl who doesn't relinquish,
A girl who likes to flog a dead horse,
A girl who likes dogs that bark at her world,
Mapule an orphan,
Mapule a lisp girl,
Mapule a natural girl.

ACTIVITIES(QUESTIONS)

1. What gender is Mapule?
2. What tone of speaking does Mapule speak?
3. Mapule likes to flog a dead horse.
   a) What is to flog a dead horse?
   b) What part of speech is this?
4. Mapule likes dogs that bark at her world.
   a) What does she mean?
   b) What are these dogs?
   c) To what does Mapule compare her enemies with?
5. Exquisite and Inquisitive.
   -What does these words tell you about Mapule?
6. Mapule has both parents.
   -True of false?Support your answer.
7. Mapule likes giving up.
   a) True or false?Support your answer.
   b) What is to relinquish?
8. Why does Mapule conclude by saying she is a natural girl?

63

Winter

By: Musa Masombuka

After all the shock and shame winter brings, it kills all forms of life and feelings, I wish if only it never existed because it unables us to do our daily activities.

Winter when were you born?
How is the life at your world?
What is your vocation?
Do you enjoy being like that?
Do you enjoy being hated?
People do not enjoy having you around,
You are a big spender,
You make us shiver for nothing,

Nothing good is celebrated about you,
Can't you have pity?
What have we done to deserve you?
You keep us under pressure,
We are unable to do our chores,
It's cold outside, there is snow out there.
We hide from you on a blazing fire,
But you keep following us,

Winter please . . . .
Just go back to your world.

ACTIVITIES(QUESTIONS)

1. How is winter described in the poem?
2. What temperature is winter?
3. Winter is a big spender. How?
4. Why nothing good is celebrated about winter?
5. Why people are unable to do their chores?
6. Why people shiver?
7. Why is winter not enjoyed?
8. Why winter keep following when they try to hide?
9. Give 2 forms of winter listed in the poem.